BREVILLE S
FRYER OVEN COOKBOOK

HEALTHY AND MOUTH-WATERING RECIPES TO LIVE
HEALTHIER AND HAPPIER BY MAKING FULL USE OF
YOUR AIR FRYER OVEN

Table of Contents

Introduction

The Breville Smart Fryer is one of the smart appliances for cooking. It looks like a transfer oven and also fries or cooks your food using the transfer method. The hot air revolves around the food placed on the cooking tray. The hot air circulation technology is the same as the transfer method. The heating elements are displayed on the top of the Breville Smart Deep Fryer with a full power fan. The fan helps to circulate the hot air flow evenly in the oven. This will allow you to cook your food quickly and evenly on all sides. Fry your food in much less oil. Take a tablespoon or less than a tablespoon of oil to fry and mash your food. If you want to fry a bowl of potato chips, your oven with the Breville Smart Air Fryer simply fries the potatoes in a tablespoon of oil. Makes your fries crisp on the outside and tender on the inside.

The Breville Smart Fryer is not only used to fry your food, but also to grill your favorite chicken, bake cakes and cookies, and also reheat your frozen foods. It comes with 12 smart cooking modes. These functions are toast, muffin, bake, broil, pizza, cookies, warm, hot, potato, waterproof, dehydrated, and slow cook. It works with an intelligent Element IQ system that finds the cold spot and automatically adjusts the temperature with PID temperature sensing and digital control, giving you even an accurate cooking. Smart ovens automatically adjust the wattage of the heating elements to give you more flexibility when cooking. The smart fryer oven works with double speed transfer technology; With this technique, you can cook your food faster by reducing cooking time by transferring. The smart fryer comes with a display that shows the 12 smart functions, as well as the cooking temperature and time. The smart fryer is also equipped with a built-in oven light, you can turn this light on at any time to see the cooking progress, or it can turn on automatically after the cook cycle is complete.

The Smart Deep Fryer is made from the most durable materials. The oven shell is made of reinforced stainless steel. In the smart oven, quartz is used instead of the metallic element because the quartz responds faster compared to the metallic element. Heat your oven quickly and evenly. The interior of the smart oven is lined with a non-stick coating that makes your daily cleaning process easy. To avoid burns, the oven rack is a self-extracting magnetic shelf. When you open the oven door, the shelves are automatically removed in the middle of the oven.

The Breville Smart Oven Fryer has one of the most flexible cooking appliances that are easy for everyone to handle. It is more than just a toaster that functions as a deep fryer, working pot, slow cooker, and also has the ability to dehydrate food. If air frying alone is not your main goal, this is the right choice for your kitchen. This smart oven works very well to heat food to the right temperature thanks to the transfer technology. It is one of the more expensive toaster ovens in this section. If your priority is more function, good performance, and flexibility, then the *Breville Smart Oven Fryer* is the best choice for your family.

How to Prepare the Smart Oven Before the First Use

It is necessary to empty the smart oven for 20 minutes before the first use to remove any protective substance adhering to the elements. Before testing, first, place your oven in a well-ventilated area and follow the instructions below.

1. First, remove the advertising stickers, multiple covers, or any packing material from the oven.

2. Remove the baking sheet, crumb tray, dehydrator basket or skillet, pizza tray, baking sheet, broil rack, multi-pack rack, and wash in hot water or soapy water with a cloth smooth and pat dry.

3. Take a soft, damp sponge to clean the inside of the oven and dry it well.

4. Place your oven in a well-ventilated area, making sure it is at least 4-6 inches apart on both sides of the oven.

5. Now insert the crumb tray into the oven in place and plug the power cord into an electrical outlet.

6. The oven display will illuminate with an alarm sound, and the function menu will appear, and the default display is in the TOAST menu setting.

7. Now turn the SELECT/CONFIRM dial until the pointer reaches the PIZZA setting.

8. Press the START/STOP button. After pressing this button, the button's backlight glows red, and the digital oven display glows orange with an audible alert.

9. The display shows the heating flashing. After healing is complete, the oven alarms and timer automatically start measurements.

10. After completing the beeping oven cycle warning, turn off the START/STOP backlight, and the oven LCD display will turn white. This will indicate that the oven is ready for its first use.

Benefits of the Air Fryer

The smart fryer oven comes with several benefits, some of which are as follows:

Healthy and Fatty Foods

The smart fryer oven works with transfer technology. Blow hot air into the cooking pan to cook food quickly and evenly on all sides. When frying your food in a smart fryer, you need a tablespoon or less than a tablespoon of oil. One bowl of fries requires only one tablespoon of oil and makes the fries crisp on the outside and tender on the inside. If you are among the people who like fried food but are worried about extra calories, this kitchen appliance is for you.

Offers 13-in-1 Operation

The Breville smart air fryer oven offers 13 functions in one device. These functions are Toast, Bagel, Bake, Broil, Hot, Pizza, Proof, Air Fry, Reheat, Cookie, Slow Cook, and Dehydrate. These are all smart programs that offer flexible cooking.

Safe to Use

The smart fryer oven cooking appliances is one of the safest compared to a traditional one. While cooking your food, the appliance is closed on all sides; because of this, there is no risk of hot oil splashing on your finger. This is one of the safest frying methods compared to another traditional frying method. A narrow cooking method gives you a splatter-free cooking experience. Smart IQ technology makes the device safer, and there is no possibility of burning food. Smart IQ automatically detects and adjusts the temperature of the item according to the needs of the recipe.

Easy to Clean

The Breville smart fryer oven is made of reinforced stainless steel, and the inner body is coated with non-stick materials. All interior accessories are dishwasher safe. You can wash it in a dishwasher or also wash it with soapy water. The smart fryer cooks your food in much less oil. Less oil means less chaos.

Care and Cleaning

1. Before starting the cleaning process, ensure that the power cord has been unplugged. Allow your oven and accessories to cool to room temperature before beginning the cleaning process.

2. Clean the oven body with a soft, damp cleaning sponge during the cleaning process. When cleaning the glass door, you can use a glass cleaner and a plastic cleaning pad to clean. Do not use metal coatings that can scratch the surface of your oven.

3. The inner body of the oven consists of a non-stick coating. Use a soft, damp sponge to clean the inside of the oven. Apply detergent to a sponge and do not apply it directly to the body of the oven. You can also use a mild spray solution to avoid staining.

4. Before cleaning the components, make sure the oven has cooled down to room temperature and then wipe gently with a soft damp cloth or sponge.

5. Dust the crumb tray with a soft, damp sponge. You can use a non-abrasive liquid cleaner. Apply detergent to a sponge and clean the disc.

6. To clean a frying pan, immerse it in warm soapy water and wash it with the help of a plastic frying pan or a soft sponge.

7. Remember to always dry all accessories thoroughly before placing them in the oven. Put the crumb tray in place before plugging the oven into its socket. Now your oven is ready for the next use.

How to Use the Breville Smart Air Fryer Oven

Your air fryer oven really couldn't be easier to use. The front opening door allows you access to the racks, which slide in and out to provide easy access to your food before, during, and after cooking.

- Remove the toaster oven from the box.

- Place it on a level surface near a grounded power outlet.

- Plug in the toaster oven

- Remove the trays from the oven. (Before using the oven make sure to thoroughly clean the trays with soap and water.)

- Set the oven to the Pizza function and use the Time button to select 18 minutes. Press the Start button and allow to finish the cooking cycle. Once the cooking cycle has finished, your Breville Mini Smart Oven is ready to use.

Learning the Controls

The great thing about the Breville Mini Smart Oven is that all of the controls are labeled for easy use, so you don't have to bother with confusing dials. Let's take a look at how the Breville Mini Smart Oven works.

Function knob: This knob allows you to select which cooking program you would like. Choose from Toast, Bake, Broil, Roast, Cookies, Reheat, Pizza, and Bagel.

LCD display: Displays the number of pieces of bread, darkness setting, current time, cooking temperature, and amount of time left to cook.

• Temp/Darkness button: Select the temperature or darkness setting for toast.

• Up and Down selection buttons: Use to adjust the time, temperature, and amount of darkness.

• Time/Slices button: Use to adjust the cooking time and number of slices of bread.

A Bit More: Adds a small amount of cooking time. The amount of time varies depending on which cooking program you have chosen.

Start/Cancel button: Starts and stops the cooking process.

• F/C button: Choose Fahrenheit or Celsius.

• Frozen Foods button: Adds extra time to the cooking process in order to defrost frozen foods.

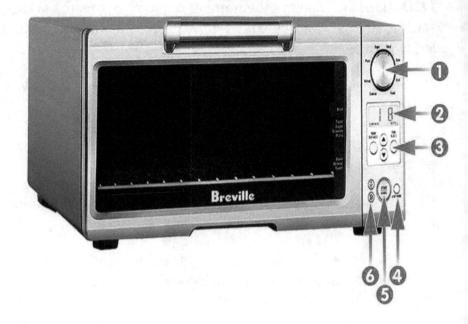

The Cooking Process

The Breville Mini Smart Oven is one of the most advanced toaster ovens on the planet due to its digital controls and Element IQ technology, which regulates the heating elements for optimum results. But perhaps the best feature of the Breville Mini Smart Oven is its ability to cook using convection. Unlike regular baking, convection produces the most even heat possible by circulating the heated air. It's perfect for many different types of cooking when you want your food to be evenly cooked throughout. It's also a great way to ensure amazing results when baking.

From the moment you choose your cooking program, the Breville Mini Smart Oven begins heating quickly. A great feature of this oven is that it preheats so quickly. And unlike many competing toaster ovens, the Breville Mini Smart Oven allows you to cook up to 450°F, which allows you to cook many foods you would not be able to in other toaster ovens. When the oven finishes cooking, its timer will chime, and it will automatically turn itself off. That's not just a great way to save energy, it's also an important safety feature. After the oven has had a chance to cool, clean it using a damp cloth or sponge to remove any spatter that may have occurred during the cooking process.

Workarounds

We've already explored many of the things your Breville Mini Smart Oven can do, so now let's talk a little about problem solving. When you're cooking in a conventional oven, it is pretty common to line your baking sheets with aluminum foil. It's a great way to keep those baking trays from getting dirty, and that's pretty helpful after your meal. But using aluminum foil in the Breville Mini Smart Oven is not a good idea. The problem is that using aluminum foil in the Breville Mini Smart Oven can cause the oven to get too hot - sometimes over 500°F - and a toaster oven, unlike your conventional oven, isn't designed to safely work at such a high temperature. To combat this problem and still have a way to line the trays of your toaster oven, try using parchment paper. It will keep food from sticking to the trays, and you can just throw it out after cooking.

You may have noticed that the Breville Mini Smart Oven features a large cooking space inside the oven. As a result, you can cook more efficiently by cooking on several levels at once. While only one cooking rack is included with the oven, you can purchase additional racks. Just make sure to purchase racks in the correct size.

Often, you will see packaged foods with a different temperature recommendation for cooking food in toaster ovens. However, because the Breville Mini Smart Oven cooks almost exactly like a regular oven, it is usually not necessary to use the recommended toaster oven temperature setting. Doing this may actually cause your food to come out overcooked. We suggest that you reduce all toaster oven temperature recommendations by twenty-five degrees to avoid overcooking.

Tips for Using Your Air fryer

One of the main problems facing families today is the excessive consumption of processed foods and fast foods, which are often high in fat, sugar, and preservatives. One of the best ways to deal with this problem is by learning how to prepare healthy meals at home, but the problem is that cooking at home can be time consuming and requires a lot of equipment. This is where your Breville smart mini-oven comes in. Because it is so easy to use and clean, cooking at home is no longer a problem.

Breville Mini Smart Oven controls are easy to use that even a beginner can become a seasoned home cook in no time. After learning how it works, the whole family will want to join in the fun of cooking quick, easy, and most importantly, healthy meals.

Preparing to Cook

- For the best final result, pat off any excess moisture from the foods. This includes meat that has been soaked in a marinade and foods that have a high level of moisture, such as potatoes.

- You need very little oil when you cook with your air fryer, and some food will not require any oil at all. However, if you are not using any oil, it is a good idea to use a little non-stick cooking spray applied directly to the food or the basket. This will help prevent your creation from sticking to the basket.

- When cutting an ingredient, try to keep the pieces uniform in size; this will ensure even cooking.

- Double check to make sure any fat drippings have been removed from the bottom of the air fryer after the previous use. Allowing fats and oils to accumulate will cause spattering and create smoke.

- When placing foods in the air fryer, remember to place them, so there is plenty of room for air to circulate, even if it means cooking in batches. This will protect the quality of the finished dish and ensure even and proper cooking.

- Preheat the air fryer by setting it to the desired cooking temperature at least three to five minutes before you plan to start cooking.

During Cooking

- Note that recipes and cooking times are an approximation. Your pieces of meat, vegetables, etc. might be a different size, or you may wish to alter the amounts of the ingredients. You might also prefer a different level of doneness. Adjust the cooking times up or down depending on the alterations you make or to suit your individual taste. How closely packed the food is in the air fryer will also impact the amount of time needed for the dish to fully cook.

- Halfway through the cooking time, rotate your food. For smaller items such as fries, this means simply shaking the basket. Larger items should be flipped over.

Always Remember

The air fryer can add an exciting new element to your culinary repertoire. There is no reason you need to stick to traditional "fried" foods. This book will introduce you to additional dishes that can be created in your air fryer. This appliance is meant to be a healthy addition to your kitchen, and with some creativity and experimentation, you can add an incredible variety of fried, roasted, steamed, and baked dishes to your list of culinary creations

Breakfast

Zucchini Squash Mix

Preparation Time: 10 minutes

Cooking Time: 35 minutes

Servings: 2

Ingredients:

- 1 lb zucchini, sliced
- 1 tbsp parsley, chopped
- 1 yellow squash, halved, deseeded, and chopped
- 1 tbsp olive oil
- Pepper
- Salt

Directions:

1   Add all ingredients into the large bowl and mix well.

2 Transfer bowl mixture into the air fryer basket and cook at 400 F for 35 minutes.

3 Serve and enjoy.

Nutrition:

Calories: 49

Fat: 3 g

Carbohydrates: 4 g

Sugar: 2 g

Protein: 1.5 g

Cholesterol: 0 mg

Special Corn Flakes Casserole

Preparation Time: 10 minutes

Cooking Time: 18 Minutes

Servings: 5

Ingredients:

- 1/3 cup milk

- 1 tbsp. cream cheese; whipped

- 1/4 tsp. nutmeg; ground

- 1/4 cup blueberries

- 1 ½ cups corn flakes; crumbled

- 3 tsp. sugar

- 2 eggs; whisked

- bread slices

Directions:

1 In a bowl, mix eggs with sugar, nutmeg, and milk and whisk well.

2 In another bowl, mix cream cheese with blueberries and whisk well.

3   Put corn flakes in a third bowl.

4   Spread blueberry mix on each bread slice; then dip in eggs mix and dredge in corn flakes at the end.

5   Place bread in your air fryer's basket; heat up at 400 °F and bake for 8 minutes.

6   Divide among plates and serve for breakfast.

Nutrition:

Calories: 300;

Fat: 5;

Fiber: 7;

Carbs: 16;

Protein: 4

Protein Rich Egg White Omelet

Preparation Time: 10 minutes

Cooking Time: 25 Minutes

Servings: 4

Ingredients:

- 1 cup egg whites

- 1/4 cup mushrooms; chopped

- 2 tbsp. chives; chopped

- 1/4 cup tomato; chopped

- 2 tbsp. skim milk

- Salt and black pepper to the taste

Directions:

1. In a bowl, mix egg whites with tomato, milk, mushrooms, chives, salt, and pepper.

2. Whisk well and pour into your air fryer's pan. Cook at 320 °F for 15 minutes.

3. Cool omelet down, slice, divide among plates, and serve.

Nutrition:

Calories: 100;

Fat: 3;

Fiber: 6;

Carbs: 7;

Carbs: 4

Shrimp Sandwiches

Preparation Time: 10 minutes

Cooking Time: 15 Minutes

Servings: 4

Ingredients:

- 1 ¼ cups cheddar; shredded
- 2 tbsp. green onions; chopped.
- whole wheat bread slices
- oz. canned tiny shrimp; drained
- 1 tbsp. mayonnaise
- 2 tbsp. butter; soft

Directions:

1 In a bowl, mix shrimp with cheese, green onion, and mayo and stir well.

2 Spread this on half of the bread slices; top with the other bread slices, cut into halves diagonally, and spread butter on top.

3 Place sandwiches in your air fryer and cook at 350 °F for 5 minutes. Divide shrimp sandwiches between plates and serve them for breakfast.

Nutrition:

Calories: 162;

Fat: 3;

Fiber: 7;

Carbs: 12; Protein: 4

Breakfast Soufflé

Preparation Time: 10 minutes

Cooking Time: 18 Minutes

Servings: 4

Ingredients:

- 4 eggs; whisked

- 1 tbsp. heavy cream

- 2 tbsp. parsley; chopped.

- 2 tbsp. chives; chopped.

- A pinch of red chili pepper; crushed

- Salt and black pepper to the taste

Directions:

1. In a bowl, mix eggs with salt, pepper, heavy cream, red chili pepper, parsley, and chives; stir well and divide into 4 soufflé dishes.

2. Arrange dishes in your air fryer and cook soufflés at 350 °F for 8 minutes. Serve them hot.

Nutrition: Calories:

300; Fat: 7;

Fiber: 9;

Carbs: 15;

Protein: 6

Fried Tomato Quiche

Preparation Time: 10 minutes

Cooking Time: 40 Minutes

Servings: 1

Ingredients:

- 1 tbsp. yellow onion; chopped.

- 1/2 cup gouda cheese; shredded

- 1/4 cup tomatoes; chopped.

- 2 eggs

- 1/4 cup milk

- Salt and black pepper to the taste

- Cooking spray

Directions:

1   Grease a ramekin with cooking spray.

2   Crack eggs, add onion, milk, cheese, tomatoes, salt, and pepper, and stir. Add this to your air fryer's pan and cook at 340 °F for 30 minutes.

Nutrition:

Calories: 241;

Fat: 6;

Fiber: 8;

Carbs: 14;

Protein: 6

Breakfast Spanish Omelet

Preparation Time: 10 minutes

Cooking Time: 20 Minutes

Servings: 4

Ingredients:

- eggs

- 1/2 chorizo; chopped

- 1 tbsp. parsley; chopped.

- 1 tbsp. feta cheese; crumbled

- 1 potato; peeled and cubed

- 1/2 cup corn

- 1 tbsp. olive oil

- Salt and black pepper to the taste

Directions:

1 Heat up your air fryer at 350 °F and add oil.

2 Add chorizo and potatoes; stir and brown them for a few seconds.

3 In a bowl, mix eggs with corn, parsley, cheese, salt and pepper, and whisk.

4   Pour this over chorizo and potatoes; spread and cook for 5 minutes. Divide omelet between plates and serve for breakfast.

Nutrition:

Calories: 300;

Fat: 6;

Fiber: 9;

Carbs: 12;

Protein: 6

Lunch

Chicken Pot Pie

Preparation Time: 10 minutes

Cooking Time: 17 minutes

Servings: 6

Ingredients

- 1 tbsp. olive oil
- 1-pound chicken breast cubed
- 1 tbsp. garlic powder
- 1 tbsp. thyme
- 1 tbsp. pepper
- 1 cup chicken broth
- oz. bag frozen mixed vegetables
- large potatoes cubed
- oz. Can cream of chicken soup
- 1 cup heavy cream
- 1 pie crust

- 1 egg 1 tbsp. water

Directions

1   Hit Sauté on the Breville smart Crispy and add chicken and olive oil.

2   Sauté chicken for 5 minutes, then stir in spices.

3   Pour in the broth along with vegetables and cream of chicken soup

4   Put on the pressure-cooking lid and seal it.

5   Hit the "Pressure Button" and select 10 minutes of cooking time, then press "Start."

6   Once the Breville smart beeps, do a quick release and remove its lid.

7   Remove the lid and stir in cream.

8   Hit sauté and cook for 2 minutes.

9   Enjoy!

Nutrition

Calories: 568 kcal/Cal

Fat: 31.1g

Carbohydrates: 50.8g

Fiber: 3.9g

Protein: 23.4g

Chicken Casserole

Preparation Time: 10 Minutes

Cooking Time: 9 minutes

Servings: 6

Ingredients

- cup chicken, shredded
- oz. bag egg noodles
- 1/2 large onion
- 1/2 cup chopped carrots
- 1/4 cup frozen peas
- 1/4 cup frozen broccoli pieces
- stalks celery chopped
- cup chicken broth
- 1 teaspoon garlic powder
- Salt and pepper to taste
- 1 cup cheddar cheese, shredded
- 1 package French's onions
- 1/4 c sour cream
- 1 can cream of chicken and mushroom soup

Directions

1 Add chicken, broth, black pepper, salt, garlic powder, vegetables, and egg noodles to the Breville smart.

2 Put on the pressure-cooking lid and seal it.

3 Hit the "Pressure Button" and select 4 minutes of cooking time, then press "Start."

4 Once the Breville smart beeps, do a quick release and remove its lid.

5 Stir in cheese, 1/3 of French's onions, can of soup, and sour cream.

6 Mix well and spread the remaining onion on top.

7 Put on the Air Fryer lid and seal it.

8 Hit the "Air fryer Button" and select 5 minutes of cooking time, then press "Start."

9 Once the Breville smart beeps, remove its lid.

10 Serve.

Nutrition

Calories: 494 kcal/Cal

Fat: 19.1g

Carbohydrates: 29g

Fiber: 2.6g

Protein: 48.9g

Ranch Chicken Wings

Preparation Time: 10 minutes

Cooking Time: 35 minutes

Servings: 6

Ingredients

- chicken wings

- 1 tablespoon olive oil

- 1 cup chicken broth

- 1/4 cup butter

- 1/2 cup Red Hot Sauce

- 1/4 teaspoon Worcestershire sauce

- 1 tablespoon white vinegar

- 1/4 teaspoon cayenne pepper

- 1/8 teaspoon garlic powder

- Seasoned salt to taste

- Ranch dressing for dipping Celery for garnish

Directions

1   Set the Air Fryer Basket in the Breville smart and pour the broth in it.

2   Spread the chicken wings in the basket and put on the pressure-cooking lid.

3   Hit the "Pressure Button" and select 10 minutes of cooking time, then press "Start."

4   Meanwhile, prepare the sauce and add butter, vinegar, cayenne pepper, garlic powder, Worcestershire sauce, and hot sauce in a small saucepan.

5   Cook this sauce for 5 minutes on medium heat until it thickens.

6   Once the Breville smart beeps, do a quick release and remove its lid.

7   Remove the wings and empty the Breville smart.

8   Toss the wings with oil, salt, and black pepper.

9   Set the Air Fryer Basket in the Breville smart and arrange the wings in it.

10 Put on the Air Fryer lid and seal it.

11 Hit the "Air Fryer Button" and select 20 minutes of cooking time, then press "Start."

12 Once the Breville smart air fryer beeps, remove its lid.

13 Transfer the wings to the sauce and mix well.

14 Serve.

Nutrition

Calories: 414

Fat: 31.6g

Carbohydrates 11.2g

Fiber: 0.3g

Protein: 20.4g

Tofu Sushi Burrito

Preparation Time: 5 minutes

Cooking Time: 15 minutes

Servings: 2

Ingredients

- ¼ block extra firm tofu, pressed and sliced
- 1 tbsp. low-sodium soy sauce
- ¼ tsp. ground ginger
- ¼ tsp. garlic powder
- Sriracha sauce, to taste
- 2 cups cooked sushi rice
- sheets nori

Filling:

- ¼ avocado, sliced
- 1 tbsp mango, sliced
- 1 green onion, finely chopped
- 1 tbsp. pickled ginger
- 2 tbsp. panko breadcrumbs

Directions

1. Whisk ginger, garlic, soy sauce, sriracha sauce, and tofu in a large bowl.

2. Let them marinate for 10 minutes, then transfer them to the air fryer basket.

3. Return the fryer basket to the air fryer and cook on air fry mode for 15 minutes at 370°F.

4. Toss the tofu cubes after 8 minutes, then resume cooking.

5. Spread a nori sheet on a work surface and top it with a layer of sushi rice.

6. Place tofu and half of the other filling ingredients over the rice.

7. Roll the sheet tightly to secure the filling inside.

8. Repeat the same steps to make another sushi roll.

9. Enjoy!

Nutrition

Calories: 372 kcal/Cal

Fat: 11.8 g

Carbohydrates: 45.8 g

Fiber: 0.6 g

Protein: 34 g

Rosemary Brussels Sprouts

Preparation Time: 5 minutes

Cooking Time: 13 minutes

Servings: 2

Ingredients

- 1 tbsp. olive oil

- garlic cloves, minced

- ½ tsp. salt

- ¼ tsp. pepper

- 1 lb. Brussels sprouts, trimmed and halved

- ½ cup panko breadcrumbs

- 1 ½ tsp. fresh rosemary, minced

Directions

1 Let your air fryer preheat at 350°F.

2 Mix oil, garlic, salt, and pepper in a bowl and heat for 30 seconds in the microwave.

3 Add 2 tablespoons of this mixture to the Brussels sprouts in a bowl and mix well to coat.

4 Spread the sprouts in the air fryer basket.

5   Return the fryer basket to the air fryer and cook on air fry mode for 5 minutes at 220°F.

6   Toss the sprouts well and continue air frying for 8 minutes more.

7   Mix the remaining oil mixture with rosemary and bread-crumbs in a bowl.

8   Spread this mixture over the Brussels sprouts and return the basket to the fryer.

9   Air fry them for 5 minutes.

10 Enjoy.

Nutrition

Calories: 246 kcal/Cal

Fat: 7.4 g

Carbohydrates: 9.4 g

Fiber: 2.7 g

Protein: 37.2 g

Dinner

Braised Sour Pork Filet

Preparation Time: 10 minutes

Cooking Time: 8 hours

Servings: 6

Ingredients:

- 1/2 tsp. of dry thyme

- 1/2 tsp. of sage

- Salt and ground black pepper to taste

- Tabs of olive oil

- lbs. of pork fillet

- 1/3 cup of shallots (chopped)

- cloves of garlic (minced)

- 3/4 cup of bone broth

- 1/3 cup of apple cider vinegar

Directions:

1. In a small bowl, combine thyme, sage, salt, and black ground pepper.

2. Rub generously pork from all sides.

3. Heat the olive oil in a large frying pan, and sear pork for 2 - 3 minutes.

4. Place pork in your Crock Pot and add shallots and garlic.

5. Pour broth and apple cider vinegar/juice.

6. Cover and cook on SLOW for 8 hours or on HIGH for 4-5 hours.

7. Remove pork on a plate, adjust salt and pepper, slice, and serve with cooking juice.

Nutrition:

Calories: 348 kcal/Cal

Carbohydrates: 3 g

Proteins: 51 g

Fat: 12.5 g

Fiber: 0.1 g

Pork with Anise and Cumin Stir-fry

Preparation Time: 5 minutes

Cooking Time: 30 minutes

Servings: 4

Ingredients:

- 1 Tbsp. lard

- spring onions finely chopped (only green part)

- cloves garlic, finely chopped

- 2 lbs. pork loin, boneless, cut into cubes

- Sea salt and black ground pepper to taste

- 1 green bell pepper (cut into thin strips)

- 1/2 cup water

- 1/2 tsp. dill seeds

- 1/2 anise seeds

- 1/2 tsp. cumin

Directions:

1. Heat the lard n a large frying pot over medium-high heat.

2. Sauté the spring onions and garlic with a pinch of salt for 3 - 4 minutes.

3. Add the pork and simmer for about 5 - 6 minutes.

4. Add all remaining ingredients and stir well.

5. Cover and let simmer for 15 - 20 minutes

6. Taste and adjust seasoning to taste.

7. Serve!

Nutrition:

Calories: 351 kcal/Cal

Carbohydrates: 3 g

Proteins: 1 g

Fat: 51.5 g

Fiber: 1 g

Baked Meatballs with Goat Cheese

Preparation Time: 15 minutes

Cooking Time: 35 minutes

Servings: 8

Ingredients:

- 1 Tbsp. of tallow

- lbs. of ground beef

- 1 organic egg

- 1 grated onion

- 1/2 cup of almond milk (unsweetened)

- 1 cup of red wine

- 1/2 bunch of chopped parsley

- 1/2 cup of almond flour

- Salt and ground pepper to taste

- 1/2 Tbsp. of dry oregano

- oz. of hard goat cheese cut in cubes

Directions:

1   Preheat oven to 400°F.

2   Grease a baking pan with tallow.

3   In a large bowl, combine all ingredients except goat cheese.

4   Knead the mixture until ingredients are evenly combined.

5   Make small meatballs and place in a prepared baking dish.

6   Place one cube of cheese on each meatball.

7   Bake for 30 - 35 minutes.

8   Serve hot.

Nutrition:

Calories: 404 kcal/Cal

Carbohydrates: 2.2 g

Proteins: 25.5 g

Fat: 31 g

Fiber: 0.5 g

Parisian Schnitzel

Preparation Time: 15 minutes

Cooking Time: 10 minutes

Servings: 4

Ingredients:

- veal steaks; thin schnitzel

- Salt and ground black pepper

- 1 Tbsp. of butter

- 4 eggs from free-range chickens

- 1 Tbsp. of almond flour

Directions:

1 Season steaks with salt and pepper.

2 Heat butter in a large nonstick frying pan at medium heat.

3 In a bowl, beat the eggs.

4 Add almond flour in a bowl.

5 Roll each steak in almond flour, add then, dip in beaten eggs.

6 Fry about 3 minutes per side.

7 Serve right away.

Nutrition:

Calories: 355 kcal/Cal

Carbohydrates: 0.3 g

Proteins: 54 g

Fat: 15 g

Fiber: 0 g

Keto Beef Stroganoff

Preparation Time: 5 minutes

Cooking Time: 30 minutes

Servings: 6

Ingredients:

- lbs. of rump or round steak or stewing steak
- 1 Tbsp. of olive oil
- green onions, finely chopped
- 1 grated tomato
- 1 Tbsp. ketchup (without sugar)
- 1 cup of button mushrooms
- 1/2 cup of bone broth
- 1 cup of sour cream

- Salt and black pepper to taste

Directions:

1. Cut the meat into strips and sauté in a large frying skillet.

2. Add chopped onion and a pinch of salt and cook meat for about 20 minutes at medium temperature.

3. Add mushrooms and ketchup and stir for 3 - 5 minutes.

4. Pour the bone broth and sour cream and cook for 3 - 4 minutes.

5. Remove from the heat, taste, and adjust salt and pepper to taste.

6. Serve hot.

Nutrition:

Calories: 348 kcal/Cal

Carbohydrates: 4.2 g

Proteins: 37 g

Fat: 21 g

Fiber: 1 g

Mains

Chicken Corn Casserole

Preparation Time: 10 minutes

Cooking Time: 40 Minutes

Servings: 6

Ingredients:

- 1 cup clean chicken stock

- oz. canned coconut milk

- 1 ½ cups green lentils

- lbs. chicken breasts; skinless, boneless, and cubed

- 1/3 cup cilantro; chopped

- 2 cups corn

- handfuls spinach

- green onions; chopped

- 1 tsp. garlic powder

- Salt and black pepper to the taste

Directions:

1. In a pan that fits your air fryer, mix stock with coconut milk, salt, pepper, garlic powder, chicken, and lentils.

2. Add corn, green onions, cilantro, and spinach; stir well,

3. introduce in your air fryer and cook at 350 °F for 30 minutes.

Nutrition:

Calories: 345;

Fat: 12;

Fiber: 10;

Carbs: 20;

Protein: 44

Veggie Toasts

Preparation Time: 10 minutes

Cooking Time: 25 Minutes

Servings: 4

Ingredients:

- 1 red bell pepper; cut into thin strips

- 1 cup cremini mushrooms; sliced

- bread slices

- 1 tbsp. butter; soft

- 1 yellow squash; chopped.

- green onions; sliced

- 1 tbsp. olive oil

- 1/2 cup goat cheese; crumbled

Directions:

1 In a bowl, mix red bell pepper with mushrooms, squash, green onions, and oil, toss; transfer to your air fryer, cook them at 350 °F, for 10 minutes; shaking the fryer once and transfer them to a bowl.

2 Spread butter on bread slices; place them in the air fryer and cook them at 350 °F for 5 minutes. Divide veggie mix on each bread slice, top with crumbled cheese, and serve for lunch.

Nutrition:

Calories: 152;

Fat: 3;

Fiber: 4;

Carbs: 7;

Protein: 2

Sides

Tender Eggplant Fries

Preparation Time: 20 minutes

Cooking Time: 30 Minutes

Servings: 2

Ingredients

- 1 eggplant, sliced

- 1 tsp olive oil

- 1 tsp soy sauce

- Salt to taste

Directions

1 Preheat your Air Fryer to 400 F. Make a marinade of 1 tsp oil, soy sauce, and salt.

2 Mix well. Add in the eggplant slices and let stand for 5 minutes.

3 Place the prepared eggplant slices in your Air Fryer's cooking basket and cook for 5 minutes.

4 Serve with a drizzle of maple syrup.

Nutrition:

Calories: 202;

Fat: 6;

Fiber: 3;

Carbs: 17;

Protein: 10

Cabbage Canapes

Preparation Time: 15 minutes

Cooking Time: 30 minutes

Servings: 2

Ingredients

- 1 whole cabbage, washed and cut into rounds

- 1 cube Amul cheese

- ½ carrot, cubed

- ¼ onion, cubed

- ¼ capsicum, cubed

- Fresh basil to garnish

Directions

1 Preheat your Air Fryer to 360 F. Using a bowl, mix onion, carrot, capsicum, and cheese. Toss to coat everything evenly. Add cabbage rounds to the Air Fryer's cooking basket.

2 Top with the veggie mixture and cook for 5 minutes. Serve with a garnish of fresh basil.

Nutrition:

Calories: 202;

Fat: 6;

Fiber: 3;

Carbs: 17;

Protein: 10

Crispy Bacon with Butterbean Dip

Preparation Time: 10 minutes

Cooking Time: 20 Minutes

Servings: 2

Ingredients

- 1 -14 oz can butter beans
- 1 tbsp chives
- ½ oz feta
- Pepper to taste
- 1 tsp olive oil
- ½ oz bacon, sliced

Directions

1 Preheat your Air Fryer to 340 F. Blend beans, oil, and pepper using a blender.

2 Arrange bacon slices on your Air Fryer's cooking basket. Sprinkle chives on top and cook for 10 minutes.

3 Add feta cheese to the butter bean blend and stir.

4 Serve bacon with the dip.

Nutrition:

Calories: 202;

Fat: 6;

Fiber: 3;

Carbs: 17;

Protein: 10

Almond French Beans

Preparation Time: 25 minutes

Cooking Time: 35 minutes

Servings: 5

Ingredients

- 1 ½ pound French beans, washed and drained
- 1 tbsp salt
- 1 tbsp pepper
- ½ pound shallots, chopped
- tbsp olive oil
- ½ cup almonds, toasted

Directions

1 Preheat your Air Fryer to 400 F. Put a pan over medium heat,

2 Mix beans in hot water and boil until tender, about 5-6 minutes.

3 Mix the boiled beans with oil, shallots, salt, and pepper.

4 Add the mixture to your Air Fryer's cooking basket and cook for 20 minutes.

5 Serve with almonds and enjoy!

Nutrition:

Calories: 202;

Fat: 6;

Fiber: 3;

Carbs: 17;

Protein: 10

Poultry

Italian Chicken Bake

Preparation Time: 10 minutes

Cooking Time: 25 minutes

Servings: 6

Ingredients:

- ¾ lbs. (340.194g) Chicken breasts

- 2 tablespoons pesto sauce

- ½ (14 oz) can tomatoes, diced

- 1 cup mozzarella cheese, shredded

- 2 tablespoon fresh basil, chopped

Directions:

1 Place the flattened chicken breasts in a baking pan and top them with pesto.

2 Add tomatoes, cheese, and basil on top of each chicken piece.

3 Press the "power button" of the air fry oven and turn the dial to select the "bake" mode.

4   Press the time button and again turn the dial to set the cooking time to 25 minutes.

5   Now push the button and rotate the dial to set the temperature at 355 degrees f.

6   Once preheated, place the baking dish inside and close its lid.

7   Serve warm.

Nutrition:

Calories 537

Total fat 19.8 g

Saturated fat 1.4 g

Cholesterol 10 mg

Sodium 719 mg

Total carbs 25.1 g

Fiber 0.9 g

Sugar 1.4 g

Protein 37.8 g

Pesto Chicken Bake

Preparation Time: 10 minutes

Cooking Time: 35 minutes

Servings: 3

Ingredients

- chicken breasts

- 1 (6 oz.) Jar basil pesto

- medium fresh tomatoes, sliced

- mozzarella cheese slices

Directions:

1 Spread the tomato slices in a casserole dish and top them with chicken.

2 Add pesto and cheese on top of the chicken and spread evenly.

3 Press the "power button" of the air fry oven and turn the dial to select the "air fry" mode.

4 Press the time button and again turn the dial to set the cooking time to 30 minutes.

5 Now push the temp button and rotate the dial to set the temperature at 350 degrees f.

6 Once preheated, place the casserole dish inside and close its lid.

7   After it is baked, switch the oven to broil mode and broil for 5 minutes.

8   Serve warm.

Nutrition:

Calories 452

Total fat 4 g

Saturated fat 2 g

Cholesterol 65 mg

Sodium 220 mg

Total carbs 23.1 g

Fiber 0.3 g

Sugar 1 g

Protein 26g

Baked Duck

Preparation Time: 10 minutes

Cooking Time: 20 minutes

Servings: 6

Ingredients

- 1 ½ sprig of fresh rosemary

- ½ nutmeg

- Black pepper

- Juice from 1 orange

- 1 whole duck

- cloves garlic, chopped

- 1 ½ red onions, chopped

- A few stalks celery

- 1 ½ carrot

- piece fresh ginger

- 1 ½ bay leaves

- lbs. (907.185g) Piper potatoes

- 2 cups chicken stock

Directions:

1. Place duck in a large cooking pot and add broth along with all the ingredients.

2. Cook this duck for 2 hours on a simmer, then transfer to the baking tray.

3. Press the "power button" of the air fry oven and turn the dial to select the "air fry" mode.

4. Press the time button and again turn the dial to set the cooking time to 20 minutes.

5. Now push the temp button and rotate the dial to set the temperature at 350 degrees f.

6. Once preheated, place the baking tray inside and close its lid.

7. Serve warm.

Nutrition:

Calories 308

Total fat 20.5 g

Saturated fat 3 g

Cholesterol 42 mg

Sodium 688 mg

Total carbs 40.3 g

Sugar 1.4 g

Fiber 4.3 g

Protein 49 g

Chicken Fajita Skewers

Preparation Time: 10 minutes

Cooking Time: 8 minutes

Servings: 2

Ingredients

- 1 lb. (453.592g) Chicken breasts, diced
- 1 tablespoon lemon juice
- 1 teaspoon chili powder
- 1 teaspoon cumin
- 1 orange bell pepper, cut into squares
- 1 red bell pepper, cut into squares
- 1 tablespoon olive oil
- 1 teaspoon garlic powder
- 1 large red onion, cut into squares
- 1 teaspoon salt
- 1 teaspoon ground black pepper
- 1 teaspoon oregano
- 1 teaspoon parsley flakes
- 1 teaspoon paprika

Directions:

1. Toss chicken and veggies with all the spices and seasoning in a bowl.

2. Alternatively, thread them on skewers and place these skewers in the air fryer basket.

3. Press the "power button" of the air fry oven and turn the dial to select the "air fry" mode.

4. Press the time button and again turn the dial to set the cooking time to 8 minutes.

5. Now push the temp button and rotate the dial to set the temperature at 360 degrees f.

6. Once preheated, place the baking dish inside and close its lid.

7. Flip the skewers when cooked halfway through, then resume cooking.

8. Serve warm.

Nutrition:

Calories 392

Total fat 16.1 g

Saturated fat 2.3 g

Cholesterol 231 mg

Sodium 466 mg

Total carbs 13.9 g

Sugar 0.6 g

Fiber 0.9 g

Protein 48 g

Zucchini Chicken Kebabs

Preparation Time: 10 minutes

Cooking Time: 16 minutes

Servings: 4

Ingredients

- 1 large zucchini, cut into squares

- chicken breasts boneless, skinless, cubed

- 1 onion yellow, cut into squares

- 1.5 cup grape tomatoes

- 1 clove garlic minced

- 1 lemon juiced

- 1/4 c olive oil

- 1 tablespoon olive oil

- 1 tablespoon red wine vinegar

- 1 teaspoon oregano

Directions:

1 Toss chicken and veggies with all the spices and seasoning in a bowl.

2 Alternatively, thread them on skewers and place these skewers in the air fryer basket.

3   Press the "power button" of the air fry oven and turn the dial to select the "air fry" mode.

4   Press the time button and again turn the dial to set the cooking time to 16 minutes.

5   Now push the temp button and rotate the dial to set the temperature at 380 degrees f.

6   Once preheated, place the baking dish inside and close its lid.

7   Flip the skewers when cooked halfway through, then resume cooking.

8   Serve warm.

Nutrition:

Calories 321

Total fat 7.4 g

Saturated fat 4.6 g

Cholesterol 105 mg

Sodium 353 mg

Total carbs 19.4 g

Sugar 6.5 g

Fiber 2.7 g

Protein 37.2 g

Chicken Soy Skewers

Preparation Time: 10 minutes

Cooking Time: 7 minutes

Servings: 4

Ingredients

- 1-lb. (453.592g) Boneless chicken tenders, diced

- 1/2 cup soy sauce

- 1/2 cup pineapple juice

- 1/4 cup sesame seed oil

- garlic cloves, chopped

- scallions, chopped

- 1 tablespoon grated ginger

- 2 teaspoons toasted sesame seeds

- Black pepper

Directions:

1   Toss chicken with all the sauces and seasonings in a baking pan.

2   Press the "power button" of the air fry oven and turn the dial to select the "air fry" mode.

3   Press the time button and again turn the dial to set the cooking time to 7 minutes.

4   Now push the temp button and rotate the dial to set the temperature at 390 degrees f.

5   Once preheated, place the baking dish inside and close its lid.

6   Serve warm.

Nutrition:

Calories 248

Total fat 15.7 g

Saturated fat 2.7 g

Cholesterol 75 mg

Sodium 94 mg

Total carbs 31.4 g

Fiber 0.4 g

Sugar 3.1 g

Protein 24.9 g

Vegetables

Crispy Jalapeno Coins

Preparation Time: 10 minutes

Cooking Time: 10 minutes

Servings: 8 to 10

Ingredients:

- 1 egg

- 2-3 tbsp. coconut flour

- 1 sliced and seeded jalapeno

- Pinch of garlic powder

- Pinch of onion powder

- Pinch of Cajun seasoning (optional)

- Pinch of pepper and salt

Directions:

1   Ensure your air fryer is preheated to 400 degrees.

2   Mix together all dry ingredients.

3   Pat jalapeno slices dry. Dip coins into egg wash and then into dry mixture. Toss to thoroughly coat.

4   Add coated jalapeno slices to air fryer in a singular layer. Spray with olive oil.

5   Cook just till crispy.

Nutrition:

Calories: 128

Fat: 8g

Protein: 7g

Sugar: 0g

Buffalo Cauliflower

Preparation Time: 15 minutes

Cooking Time: 14 to 17 minutes

Servings: 6 to 8

Ingredients:

Cauliflower:

- 1 C. panko breadcrumbs

- 1 tsp. salt

- C. cauliflower florets

Buffalo Coating:

- ¼ C. Vegan Buffalo sauce

- ¼ C. melted vegan butter

Directions:

1 Melt butter in microwave and whisk in buffalo sauce.

2 Dip each cauliflower floret into buffalo mixture, ensuring it gets coated well. Hold over a bowl till floret is done dripping.

3 Mix breadcrumbs with salt.

4 Dredge dipped florets into breadcrumbs and place into the air fryer.

5 Cook 14-17 minutes at 350 degrees. When slightly browned, they are ready to eat!

6 Serve with your favorite keto dipping sauce!

Nutrition:

Calories: 194

Fat: 17g

Protein: 10g

Sugar: 3g

Jicama Fries

Preparation Time: 10 minutes

Cooking Time: 20 minutes

Servings: 8

Ingredients:

- 1 tbsp. dried thyme

- ¾ C. arrowroot flour

- ½ large Jicama

- 4 eggs

Directions:

1 Sliced jicama into fries.

2 Whisk eggs together and pour over fries. Toss to coat.

3 Mix a pinch of salt, thyme, and arrowroot flour together. Toss egg-coated jicama into dry mixture, tossing to coat well.

4 Spray air fryer basket with olive oil and add fries. Cook 20 minutes on CHIPS setting. Toss halfway into the cooking process.

Nutrition:

Calories: 211

Fat: 19g

Protein: 9g Sugar: 1g

Air Fryer Brussels Sprouts

Preparation Time: 5 minutes

Cooking Time: 10 minutes

Servings: 5

Ingredients:

- ¼ tsp. salt

- 1 tbsp. balsamic vinegar

- 1 tbsp. olive oil

- C. Brussels sprouts

Directions:

1   Cut Brussels sprouts in half lengthwise. Toss with salt, vinegar, and olive oil till coated thoroughly.

2   Add coated sprouts to the air fryer, cooking 8-10 minutes at 400 degrees. Shake after 5 minutes of cooking.

3   Brussels sprouts are ready to devour when brown and crisp!

Nutrition:

Calories: 118

Fat: 9g

Protein: 11g

Sugar: 1g

Spaghetti Squash Tots

Preparation Time: 5 minutes

Cooking Time: 15 minutes

Servings: 8 to 10

Ingredients:

- ¼ tsp. pepper

- ½ tsp. salt

- 1 thinly sliced scallion

- 1 spaghetti squash

Directions:

1. Wash and cut the squash in half lengthwise. Scrape out the seeds.

2. With a fork, remove spaghetti meat by strands and throw out skins.

3. In a clean towel, toss in squash and wring out as much moisture as possible. Place in a bowl and with a knife slice the meat a few times to cut up smaller.

4. Add pepper, salt, and scallions to squash and mix well.

5. Create "tot" shapes with your hands and place in the air fryer. Spray with olive oil.

6   Cook 15 minutes at 350 degrees until golden and crispy!

Nutrition:

Calories: 231

Fat: 18g

Protein: 5g

Sugar: 0g

Cinnamon Butternut Squash Fries

Preparation Time: 10 minutes

Cooking Time: 10 minutes

Servings: 2

Ingredients:

- 1 pinch of salt

- 1 tbsp. powdered unprocessed sugar

- ½ tsp. nutmeg

- 1 tsp. cinnamon

- 1 tbsp. coconut oil

- ounces pre-cut butternut squash fries

Directions:

1. In a plastic bag, pour in all ingredients. Coat fries with other components till coated and sugar is dissolved.

2. Spread coated fries into a single layer in the air fryer. Cook 10 minutes at 390 degrees until crispy.

Nutrition:

Calories: 175

Fat: 8g

Protein: 1g

Sugar: 5g

Carrot & Zucchini Muffins

Preparation Time: 5 minutes

Cooking Time: 14 minutes

Servings: 4

Ingredients:

- 2 tablespoons butter, melted
- ¼ cup carrots, shredded
- ½ cup zucchini, shredded
- 1 ½ cups almond flour
- 1 tablespoon liquid Stevia
- 2 teaspoons baking powder
- Pinch of salt
- 4 eggs
- 1 tablespoon yogurt
- 1 cup milk

Directions:

1   Preheat your air fryer to 350°Fahrenheit.

2   Beat the eggs, yogurt, milk, salt, pepper, baking soda, and Stevia.

3 Whisk in the flour gradually.

4 Add zucchini and carrots.

5 Grease muffin tins with butter and pour the muffin batter into tins. Cook for 14-minutes and serve.

Nutrition:

Calories: 224,

Total Fats: 12.3g,

Carbs: 11.2g,

Protein: 14.2g

Beef

Beef Zucchini Shashliks

Preparation Time: 10 minutes

Cooking Time: 25 minutes

Servings: 4

Ingredients

- 1lb. (453.592g) Beef, boned and diced

- 1 lime, juiced and chopped

- tablespoon olive oil

- 20 garlic cloves, chopped

- 1 handful rosemary, chopped

- green peppers, cubed

- zucchinis, cubed

- red onions, cut into wedges

Directions:

1. Toss the beef with the rest of the skewer's ingredients in a bowl.

2. Thread the beef, peppers, zucchini, and onion on the skewers.

3. Place these beef skewers in the air fry basket.

4. Press the "power button" of the air fry oven and turn the dial to select the "air fryer" mode.

5. Press the time button and again turn the dial to set the cooking time to 25 minutes.

6. Now push the temp button and rotate the dial to set the temperature at 370 degrees f.

7. Once preheated, place the air fryer basket in the oven and close its lid.

8. Flip the skewers when cooked halfway through, then resume cooking.

9. Serve warm.

Nutrition:

Calories 472

Total fat 11.1 g

Saturated fat 5.8 g

Cholesterol 610 mg

Sodium 749 mg

Total carbs 19.9 g

Fiber 0.2 g

Sugar 0.2 g

Protein 13.5 g

Spiced Beef Skewers

Preparation Time: 10 minutes

Cooking Time: 18 minutes

Servings: 4

Ingredients

- 2 teaspoons ground cumin

- 2 teaspoons ground coriander

- 1/4 teaspoon ground cinnamon

- 1/8 teaspoon ground smoked paprika

- 2 teaspoons lime zest

- 1/2 teaspoon salt

- 1/2 teaspoon black pepper

- 1 tablespoon lemon juice

- 2 teaspoons olive oil

- 1 1/2 lbs. Lean beef, cubed

Directions:

1. Toss beef with the rest of the skewer's ingredients in a bowl.

2. Thread the beef and veggies on the skewers alternately.

3   Place these beef skewers in the air fry basket.

4   Press the "power button" of the air fry oven and turn the dial to select the "air fryer" mode.

5   Press the time button and again turn the dial to set the cooking time to 18 minutes.

6   Now push the temp button and rotate the dial to set the temperature at 370 degrees f.

7   Once preheated, place the air fryer basket in the oven and close its lid.

8   Flip the skewers when cooked halfway through, then resume cooking.

9   Serve warm.

Nutrition:

Calories 327

Total fat 3.5 g

Saturated fat 0.5 g

Cholesterol 162 mg

Sodium 142 mg

Total carbs 33.6 g

Fiber 0.4 g

Sugar 0.5 g

Protein 24.5 g

Beef Sausage with Cucumber Sauce

Preparation Time: 10 minutes

Cooking Time: 15 minutes

Servings: 6

Ingredients

- Beef kabobs

- 1 lb. (453.592g) Ground beef

- 1/2 an onion, finely diced

- garlic cloves, finely minced

- 2 teaspoons cumin

- 2 teaspoons coriander

- 1 ½ teaspoons salt

- 2 tablespoons chopped mint

Yogurt sauce:

- 1 cup Greek yogurt

- 2 tablespoons cucumber, chopped

- garlic cloves, minced

- 1/4 teaspoon salt

Directions:

1. Toss beef with the rest of the kebob ingredients in a bowl.

2. Make 6 sausages out of this mince and thread them on the skewers.

3. Place these beef skewers in the air fry basket.

4. Press the "power button" of the air fry oven and turn the dial to select the "air fryer" mode.

5. Press the time button and again turn the dial to set the cooking time to 15 minutes.

6. Now push the temp button and rotate the dial to set the temperature at 370 degrees f.

7. Once preheated, place the air fryer basket in the oven and close its lid.

8. Flip the skewers when cooked halfway through, then resume cooking.

9. Meanwhile, prepare the cucumber sauce by whisking all its ingredients in a bowl.

10. Serve the skewers with cucumber sauce.

Nutrition:

Calories 353

Total fat 7.5 g

Saturated fat 1.1 g

Cholesterol 20 mg

Sodium 297 mg

Total carbs 10.4 g

Fiber 0.2 g

Sugar 0.1 g

Protein 13.1 g

Beef Eggplant Medley

Preparation Time: 10 minutes

Cooking Time: 20 minutes

Servings: 4

Ingredients

- cloves of garlic

- 1 teaspoon dried oregano

- Olive oil

- beef steaks, diced

- eggplant, cubed

- fresh bay leaves

- lemons, juiced

- A few sprigs parsley, chopped

Directions:

1 Toss beef with the rest of the skewer's ingredients in a bowl.

2 Thread the beef and veggies on the skewers alternately.

3 Place these beef skewers in the air fry basket.

4 Press the "power button" of the air fry oven and turn the dial to select the "air fryer" mode.

5 Press the time button and again turn the dial to set the cooking time to 20 minutes.

6 Now push the temp button and rotate the dial to set the temperature at 370 degrees f.

7 Once preheated, place the air fryer basket in the oven and close its lid.

8 Flip the skewers when cooked halfway through, then resume cooking.

9 Serve warm.

Nutrition:

Calories 248

Total fat 13 g

Saturated fat 7 g

Cholesterol 387 mg

Sodium 353 mg

Total carbs 1 g

Fiber 0.4 g

Sugar 1 g

Protein 29 g

Seafood

Tuna Stuffed Potatoes

Preparation Time: 5 minutes

Cooking Time: 30 minutes

Servings: 4

Ingredients

- starchy potatoes

- ½ tablespoon olive oil

- 1 (6-ounce) can tuna, drained

- tablespoons plain greek yogurt

- 1 teaspoon red chili powder

- Salt and freshly ground black pepper to taste

- 1 scallion, chopped and divided

- 1 tablespoon capers

Directions:

1. In a large bowl of water, soak the potatoes for about 30 minutes. Drain well and pat dry with paper towel.

2. Preheat the air fryer to 355 degrees f. Place the potatoes in a fryer basket.

3. Cook for about 30 minutes.

4. Meanwhile in a bowl, add tuna, yogurt, red chili powder, salt, black pepper and half of scallion and with a potato masher, mash the mixture completely.

5. Remove the potatoes from the air fryer oven and place onto a smooth surface.

6. Carefully, cut each potato from top side lengthwise.

7. With your fingers, press the open side of potato halves slightly. Stuff the potato open portion with tuna mixture evenly.

8. Sprinkle with the capers and remaining scallion. Serve immediately.

Nutrition:

Calories: 795,

Protein: 109.77g,

Fat: g,

Carbs: g

Fried Calamari

Preparation Time: 8 minutes

Cooking Time: 7 minutes

Servings: 6-8

Ingredients

- ½ tsp. Salt

- ½ tsp. Old bay seasoning

- 1/3 c. Plain cornmeal

- ½ c. Semolina flour

- ½ c. Almond flour

- 5-6 c. Olive oil

- 1 ½ pound (680.389g) baby squid

Directions:

1. Rinse squid in cold water and slice tentacles, keeping just ¼-inch of the hood in one piece.

2. Combine 1-2 pinches of pepper, salt, old bay seasoning, cornmeal, and both flours together. Dredge squid pieces into flour mixture and place into the air fryer basket.

3. Spray liberally with olive oil. Cook 15 minutes at 345 degrees till coating turns a golden brown.

Nutrition:

calories: 211;

carbs:55;

fat: 6g;

protein:21g;

sugar:1g

Soy and Ginger Shrimp

Preparation Time: 8 minutes

Cooking Time: 10 minutes

Servings: 4

Ingredients

- 2 tablespoons olive oil

- 2 tablespoons scallions, finely chopped

- cloves garlic, chopped

- 1 teaspoon fresh ginger, grated

- 1 tablespoon dry white wine

- 1 tablespoon balsamic vinegar

- 1/4 cup soy sauce

- 1 tablespoon sugar

- 1 pound (453.592g) shrimp

- Salt and ground black pepper to taste

Directions:

1. To make the marinade, warm the oil in a saucepan; cook all ingredients, except the shrimp, salt, and black pepper. Now, let it cool.

2. Marinate the shrimp, covered, at least an hour, in the refrigerator.

3. After that, pour inside the oven rack/basket.

4. Set the rack on the middle shelf of the air fryer oven.

5. Set temperature to 350°f and set time to 10 minutes. Bake the shrimp at 350 degrees f for 8 to 10 minutes (depending on the size), turning once or twice.

6. Season prepared shrimp with salt and black pepper and serve.

Nutrition:

Calories: 233,

Protein: 24.55g,

Fat: 10.28g,

Carbs: 10.86g

Crispy Cheesy Fish Fingers

Preparation Time: 10 minutes

Cooking Time: 20 minutes

Servings: 4

Ingredients

- Large cod fish filet, approximately 6-8 ounces, fresh or frozen and thawed, cut into 1 ½-inch strips

- raw eggs

- ½ cup of breadcrumbs (we like panko, but any brand or home recipe will do)

- 2 tablespoons of shredded or powdered parmesan cheese

- 1 tablespoon of shredded cheddar cheese

- Pinch of salt and pepper

Directions:

1. Cover the basket of the air fryer oven with a lining of tin foil, leaving the edges uncovered to allow air to circulate through the basket.

2. Preheat the air fryer oven to 350 degrees.

3. In a large mixing bowl, beat the eggs until fluffy and until the yolks and whites are fully combined.

4. Dunk all the fish strips in the beaten eggs, fully submerging.

5. In a separate mixing bowl, combine the bread crumbs with the parmesan, cheddar, and salt and pepper, until evenly mixed.

6. One by one, coat the egg-covered fish strips in the mixed dry ingredients so that they're fully covered, and place on the foil-lined air fryer basket.

7. Set the air fryer oven timer to 20 minutes.

8. Halfway through the cooking time, shake the handle of the air fryer so that the breaded fish jostles inside and fry coverage is even.

9. After 20 minutes, when the fryer shuts off, the fish strips will be perfectly cooked, and their breaded crust golden-brown and delicious! Using tongs, remove from the air fryer and set on a serving dish to cool.

Nutrition:

Calories: 124,

Protein: 6.86g,

Fat: 5.93g,

Carbs: 12.26g

Panko-Crusted Tilapia

Preparation Time: 5 minutes

Cooking Time: 10 minutes

Servings: 3

Ingredients

- 2 tsp. Italian seasoning
- 1 tsp. Lemon pepper
- 1/3 c. Panko breadcrumbs
- 1/3 c. Egg whites
- 1/3 c. Almond flour
- tilapia fillets
- Olive oil

Directions:

1 Place panko, egg whites, and flour into separate bowls. Mix lemon pepper and italian seasoning in with breadcrumbs.

1. Pat tilapia fillets dry. Dredge in flour, then egg, then breadcrumb mixture.

2. Add to the air fryer basket and spray lightly with olive oil.

3. Cook 10-11 minutes at 400 degrees, making sure to flip halfway through cooking.

Nutrition:

calories: 256;

fat: 9g;

protein:39g;

sugar:5g

Potato Crusted Salmon

Preparation Time: 10 minutes

Cooking Time: 15 minutes

Servings: 4

Ingredients

- 1 pound (453.592g) salmon, swordfish, or arctic char fillets, 3/4 inch thick

- 1 egg white

- 2 tablespoons water

- 1/3 cup dry instant mashed potatoes

- 2 teaspoons cornstarch

- 1 teaspoon paprika

- 1 teaspoon lemon pepper seasoning

Directions:

1   Remove and skin from the fish and cut it into 4 serving pieces, mix together the egg white and water. Mix together all of the dry ingredients. Dip the fillets into the egg white mixture, then press into the potato mix to coat evenly.

2   Pour on the oven shelf/basket. Place the grill in the center of the frame of the pots.

3   Set temperature to 360°f, and set time to 15 minutes, flip the filets halfway through.

Nutrition:

calories:176;

fat: 7g;

protein:23g;

Snacks

Italian Corn Fritters

Preparation Time: 10 minutes

Cooking Time: 3 minutes

Servings: 4

Ingredients:

- 2 cups frozen corn kernels
- 1/3 cup finely ground cornmeal
- 1/3 cup flour
- ½ tsp. salt
- ¼ tsp. pepper
- ½ tsp. baking powder
- Onion powder, to taste
- Garlic powder, to taste
- ¼ tsp. paprika
- 1 tbsp. green chilies with juices
- 1 tbsp. almond milk

- ¼ cup chopped Italian parsley

Directions:

1 Beat cornmeal with flour, baking powder, parsley, seasonings in a bowl. Blend 3 tbsp. almond milk with 1 cup corn, black pepper, and salt in a food processor until smooth.

2 Stir in the flour mixture, then mix until smooth. Spread this corn mixture on a baking tray lined with wax paper.

3 Set the baking tray inside the Air Fryer toaster oven and close the lid.

4 Select the bake mode at 350°F temperature for 2 minutes. Slice and serve.

Nutrition:

Calories: 146 Cal

Protein: 6.3 g

Carbs: 18.8 g

Fat: 4.5 g

Artichoke Fries

Preparation Time: 8 minutes

Cooking Time: 13 minutes

Servings: 6

Ingredients:

- 1 oz. can artichoke hearts

- 1 cup flour

- 1 cup almond milk

- ½ tsp. garlic powder

- ¾ tsp. salt

- ¼ tsp. black pepper, or to taste

For Dry Mix:

- 1 ½ cup panko breadcrumbs

- ½ tsp. paprika

- ¼ tsp. salt

Directions:

1 Whisk the wet ingredients in a bowl until smooth, and mix the dry ingredients in a separate bowl.

2   First, dip the artichokes quarters in the wet mixture then coat with the dry panko mixture.

3   Place the artichokes hearts in the Air Fryer basket. Insert the basket inside the Air Fryer toaster oven and close the lid.

4   Select the Air Fry mode at 340°F temperature for 13 minutes. Serve warm.

Nutrition:

Calories: 199 Cal

Protein: 9.4 g

Carbs: 15.9 g

Fat: 4 g

Desserts

Buttery Scallops

Preparation Time: 10 minutes

Cooking Time: 25 minutes

Servings: 8

Ingredients

- lb. (907.185g) Scallops

- 2 tablespoons butter, melted

- 2 tablespoons dry white wine

- 1 tablespoon lemon juice

- 1/2 cup parmesan cheese, grated

- 1 teaspoon salt

- 1/2 teaspoon black pepper

- 1 teaspoon garlic powder

- 1 teaspoon dried parsley

- 1/8 teaspoon cayenne pepper

- 1/4 teaspoon sweet paprika

- 2 tablespoons parsley chopped

Directions:

1   Mix everything in a bowl except scallops.

2   Toss in scallops and mix well to coat them.

3   Spread the scallops with the sauce on a baking tray.

4   Press the "power button" of the air fry oven and turn the dial to select the "bake" mode.

5   Press the time button and again turn the dial to set the cooking time to 25 minutes.

6   Now push the temp button and rotate the dial to set the temperature at 350 degrees f.

7   Once preheated, place the scallop's baking tray in the oven and close its lid.

8   Serve warm.

Nutrition:

Calories 227

Total fat 10.1g

Saturated fat 5.7g

Cholesterol 89mg

Sodium 388mg

Total carbohydrate 5.6g

Dietary fiber 0.1g

Total sugars 0.2g

Protein 27.8g

Crusted Scallops

Preparation Time: 10 minutes

Cooking Time: 20 minutes

Servings: 4

Ingredients

- 1 1/2 lbs. (680.389g) Bay scallops, rinsed

- garlic cloves, minced

- 1/2 cup panko crumbs

- 1 teaspoon onion powder

- 2 tablespoons butter, melted

- 1/2 teaspoon cayenne pepper

- 1 teaspoon garlic powder

- 1/4 cup parmesan cheese, shredded

Directions:

1 Mix everything in a bowl except scallops.

2 Toss in scallops and mix well to coat them.

3 Spread the scallops with the sauce in a baking tray.

4 Press the "power button" of the air fry oven and turn the dial to select the "bake" mode.

5 Press the time button and again turn the dial to set the cooking time to 20 minutes.

6 Now push the temp button and rotate the dial to set the temperature at 400 degrees f.

7 Once preheated, place the scallop's baking tray in the oven and close its lid.

Nutrition:

Calories 242

Total fat 11.1g

Saturated fat 6.4g

Cholesterol 65mg

Sodium 500mg

Total carbohydrate 11.1g

Dietary fiber 0.7g

Total sugars 0.9g

Protein 23.8g

Lobster Tails with White Wine Sauce

Preparation Time: 10 minutes

Cooking Time: 14 minutes

Servings: 4

Ingredients

- lobster tails, shell cut from the top

- 1/2 onion, quartered

- 1/2 cup butter

- 1/3 cup wine

- 1/4 cup honey

- garlic cloves crushed

- 1 tablespoon lemon juice

- 1 teaspoon salt or to taste

- Cracked pepper to taste

- Lemon slices to serve

- tablespoons fresh chopped parsley

Directions:

1   Place the lobster tails in the oven's baking tray.

2 Whisk the rest of the ingredients in a bowl and pour over the lobster tails.

3 Press the "power button" of the air fry oven and turn the dial to select the "broil" mode.

4 Press the time button and again turn the dial to set the cooking time to 14 minutes.

5 Now push the temp button and rotate the dial to set the temperature at 350 degrees f.

6 Once preheated, place the lobster's baking tray in the oven and close its lid.

7 Serve warm.

Nutrition:

Calories 340

Total fat 23.1g

Saturated fat 14.6g

Cholesterol 61mg

Sodium 1249mg

Total carbohydrate 20.4g

Dietary fiber 0.3g

Total sugars 18.1g

Protein 0.7g

Conclusion

Hopefully, after going through this book and trying out a couple of recipes, you will get to understand the flexibility and utility of the Breville smart air fryers. It is undoubtedly a multipurpose kitchen appliance that is highly recommended to everybody as it presents one with a palatable atmosphere to enjoy fried foods that are not only delicious but healthy, cheaper, and more convenient. The use of this kitchen appliance ensures that the making of some of your favorite snacks and meals will be carried out in a stress-free manner without hassling around, which invariably legitimizes its worth and gives you value for your money.

This book will be your all-time guide to understand the basics of the Breville smart air fryer because, with all the recipes mentioned in the book, you are rest assured that it will be something that you and the rest of the people around the world will enjoy for the rest of your lives. You will be able to prepare delicious and flavorsome meals that will not only be easy to carry out, but tasty and healthy as well.

However, you should never limit yourself to the recipes solely mentioned in this cookbook, go on and try new things! Explore new recipes! Experiment with different ingredients, seasonings, and different methods! Create some new recipes and keep your mind open. By so doing, you will be able to get the best out of your Breville smart air fryer oven.

We are so glad you took the leap to this healthier cooking format with us!

The air fryer truly is not a gadget that should stay on the shelf. Instead, take it out and give it a whirl when you are whipping up one of your tried-and-true recipes or if you are starting to get your feet wet with the air frying method.

Regardless of appliances, recipes, or dietary concerns, we hope you have fun in your kitchen. Between food preparation, cooking time, and then the cleanup, a lot of time is spent in this one room, so it should be as fun as possible.

This is just the start. There are no limits to working with the Breville smart air fryer, and we will explore some more recipes as well. In addition to all the great options that we talked about before, you will find that there are tasty desserts that can make those sweet teeth in no time, and some great sauces and dressing so you can always be in control over the foods you eat. There are just so many options to choose from that it won't take long before you find a whole bunch of recipes to use, and before you start to wonder why you didn't get the Breville smart air fryer so much sooner. There are so many things to admire about the air fryer, and it becomes an even better tool to use when you have the right recipes in place and can use them. And there are so many fantastic recipes that work well in the air fryer and can get dinner on the table in no time. We are pleased that you pursue this Breville smart Air Fryer oven cookbook. Happy, healthy eating!

CPSIA information can be obtained
at www.ICGtesting.com
Printed in the USA
BVHW091011280521
608375BV00009B/1308